THE SPECTRUM OF
MUSIC
with Related Arts

A Macmillan/Schirmer program

Mary Val Marsh
Carroll Rinehart
Edith Savage

Macmillan Publishing Co., Inc.
New York

Collier Macmillan Publishers
London

Parts of this work were published in earlier editions of *The Spectrum of Music with Related Arts.*

Macmillan Publishing Co., Inc.
866 Third Avenue, New York, New York 10022
Collier Macmillan Canada, Inc.
Printed in the United States of America
ISBN 0-02-291860-4

9 8 7 6 5 4 3 2

Acknowledgments

Amadeo Music for "Marty" by Malvina Reynolds. Copyright © 1962. Amadeo Music, Hollywood, California. Used by permission. All rights reserved.

Bowmar/Noble Publishers, Inc., for "Candles of Hanukkah" from SING A SONG by Lucille Wood, Roberta McLaughlin. Copyright 1973 by Bowmar/Noble Publishers, Inc. Used by permission of Bowmar/Noble Publishers, Inc., Los Angeles, California.

E. P. Dutton & Co., Inc. for "Little Black Bug" by Margaret Wise Brown from ANOTHER HERE AND NOW STORY BOOK by Lucy Sprague Mitchell. Copyright, 1937, by E. P. Dutton & Co.; renewal © 1965 by Lucy Sprague Mitchell. Reprinted by permission.

Friendship Press for "Congo Lullaby," words by Carol Hart Sayre from THE WHOLE WORLD SINGING compiled by Edith Lovell Thomas, copyright © 1950. Used by permission.

continued on page 62

Contents

How Is Music Made?

Move over and
make room for . . .

Little Black Bug

Squeak - eak - eak - eak - eak.

Bzzzzzzzzzzzzzzzzzzzzzzzzzzzzzzzzzzzzzzzz

Bug-ug-ug-ug

ENVIRONMENTAL SOUNDS: Pitch

Make Animals

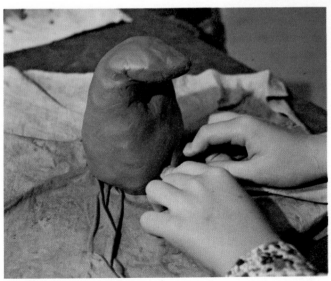

SINGING GAME: Pitch and Rhythm

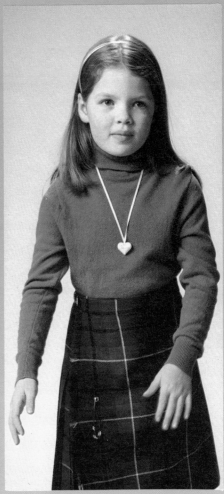

8
FOUND OBJECTS: Timbre and Pitch

What does Tony hear?

ENVIRONMENTAL SOUNDS: Timbre and Rhythm

CAUTION
HARD HAT

11

12

PLAYING DRUMS: Rhythm and Pitch

Drum Talk

A Story in Music

14

PERCUSSION INSTRUMENTS: Timbre and Rhythm

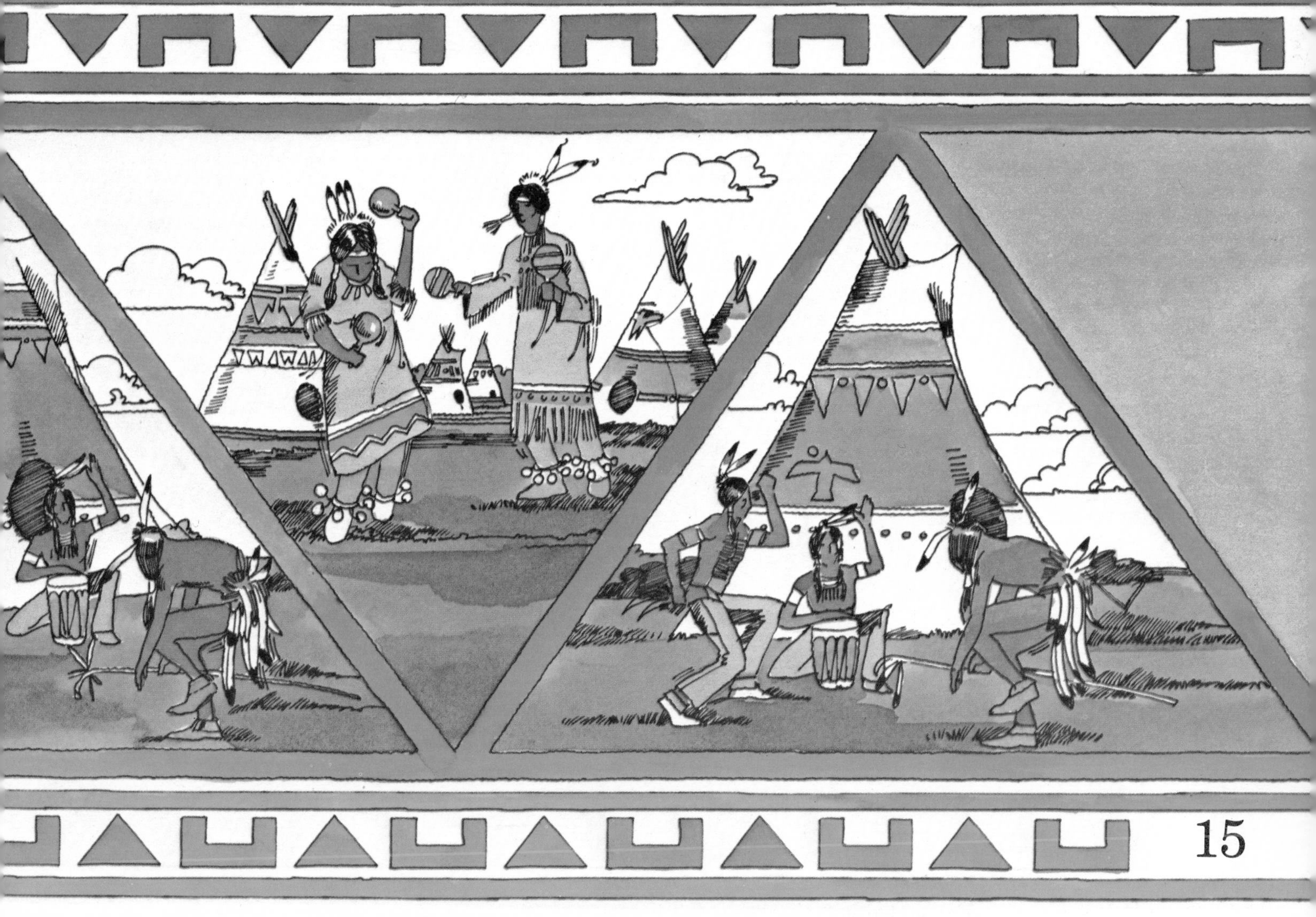

Play a Tune

```
                              A   A
           G   G                        G___

   C   C
```

```
   F   F
           E   E
                   D   D
                          C___
```

Make up a tune.

BELLS: Pitch

Trot, Pony, Trot

BELLS: Pitch

Autoharp

    F   F   F   F

Down came a lady, _____ down   came   two,

    F   F   F   F

18 Down came   Sara Ann and she was dressed in blue.

String Instruments

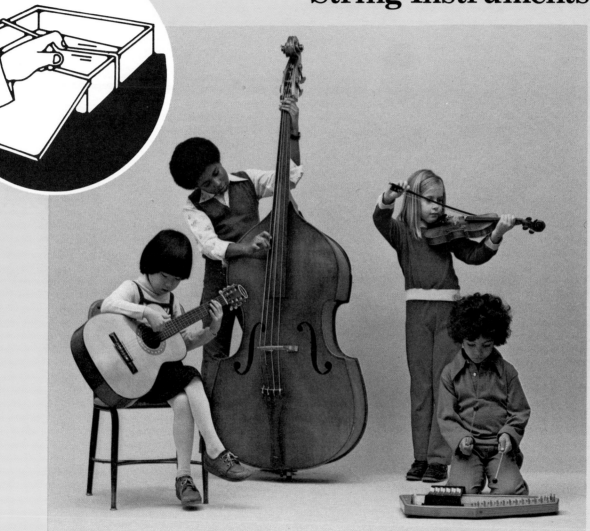

Wind Instruments

WIND INSTRUMENTS: Timbre and Pitch

BRASS INSTRUMENTS: Timbre and Rhythm

Bells in the Tower

F   F   F   F   F   F   F

Ding - dong, Ding - dong, Ding - dong, Ding!___

RHYTHM: Duration

Fray Martín

C   D E   C   F   D E   C

Fray   Mar-tín

E   F G   E   A   F G   E

C'   C'   C'   C'

Tan!   Tan!   Tan!   Tan!

23
RHYTHM: Duration

All Around the Town

Clap to
the left.

Clap to
the right.

Clap above
your head.

Then way
down low.

Clap behind
your back
and away
out of sight.

Now   it's   all   a - round   the   town,

RHYTHM: Beat

 then it's home, you know.

25

Left, Right Left, Right

RHYTHM: Beat

Ted - dy Bear, **Ted** - dy Bear,

turn a**round.**

Ted - dy Bear, **Ted** - dy Bear,

touch the **ground.**

Ted - dy Bear, **Ted** - dy Bear,

show your **shoe.**

Ted - dy Bear, **Ted** - dy Bear,

that will **do!**

27

Short Long

How does this horse move?

How does this horse move?

Low High

C′

C

Hop up

Hop Up, My Ladies

PITCHES: Low–High

High Low

C′

C

Help me!

Little Cottage in the Wood

Make Up Music

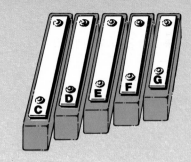

Play this tune.

G —	**G** —

C —   **C**

Jump,   jump,   jump   all   day,

End the tune.

Hur - ry   back   an - oth - er   way. _____

MELODY: Pitch Direction

Play This Tune

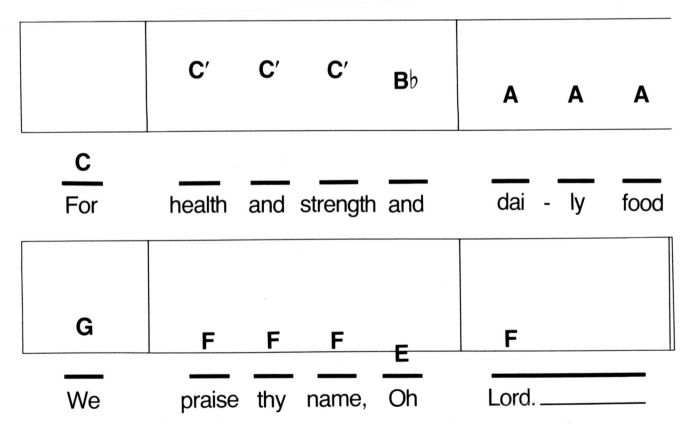

| | C′   C′   C′   B♭ | A   A   A |

C
—   —   —   —   —   —   —

For   health   and   strength   and   dai - ly   food

| | **F**   **F**   **F**   **E** | **F** |

G
—   —   —   —   —   ▬▬▬▬

We   praise   thy   name,   Oh   Lord. _____

33

Ten Puppies

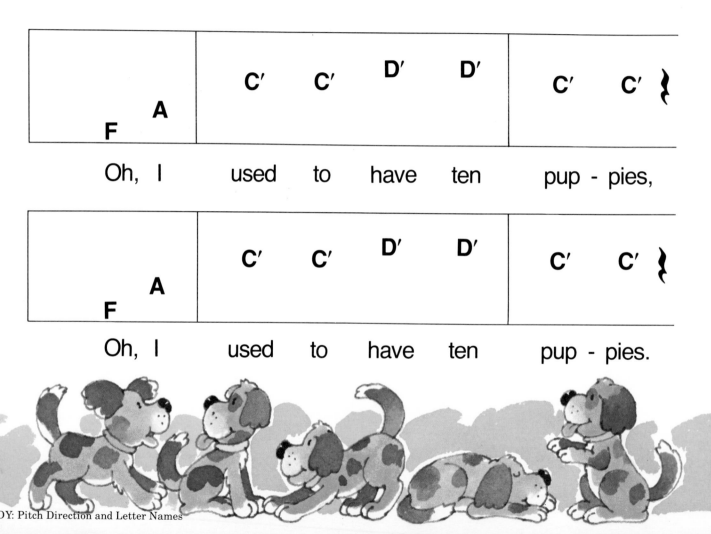

	C′ C′ D′ D′	C′ C′ ⁊
F A		

Oh, I   used   to   have   ten   pup - pies,

	C′ C′ D′ D′	C′ C′ ⁊
F A		

Oh, I   used   to   have   ten   pup - pies.

MELODY: Pitch Direction and Letter Names

C′ C′	C′ Bb A G	C′_____ ⸯ

One fell   in   the   snow   so   fine_____

C′ C′	C′ Bb A G	F_____

Leav - ing   me   with   on - ly   nine_____

Play the song.

	A **A**		**A** ♪
F **F** **F**		**F** **F**	

— — —   — —   — *rest*

Down came a　　la - dy,　　down　came　two,

			♪
	A A A	**A** **G**	
F **F**	**F**	**F** **E**	**F**

— — —   — — — — —   — *rest*

Down　came　Sa - ra　Ann and she was dressed in　blue.

Play this song with the notes.

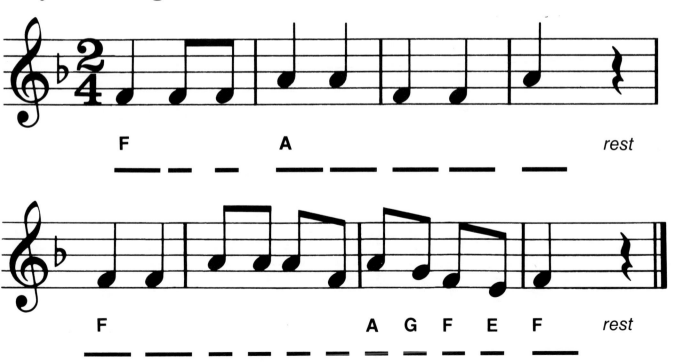

37

Hot Cross Buns

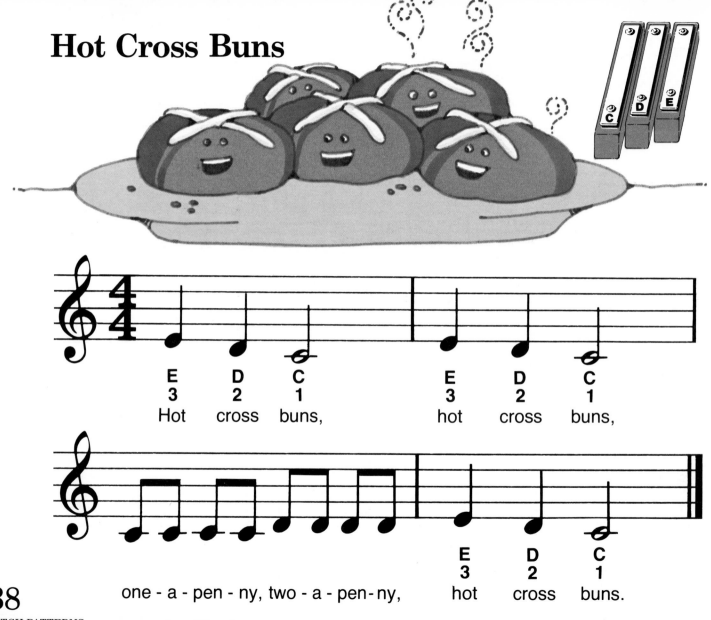

Hot cross buns,

E 3   D 2   C 1   hot cross buns,

E 3   D 2   C 1

one - a - pen - ny, two - a - pen - ny,

hot cross buns.

E 3   D 2   C 1

Bell Horses

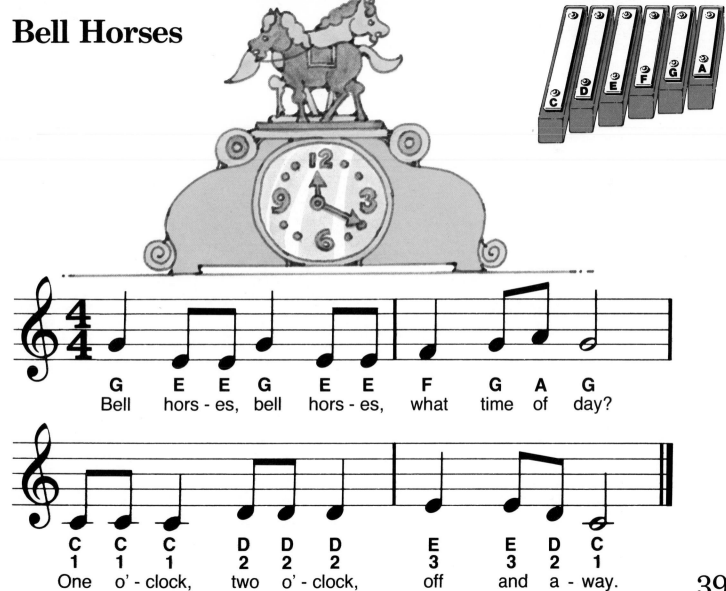

G E E G E E F G A G
Bell hors-es, bell hors-es, what time of day?

C C C D D D E E D C
1 1 1 2 2 2 3 3 2 1
One o'-clock, two o'-clock, off and a-way.

By'm Bye

By'm **C′** **C′** By'm

bye **G** **G** bye

G

C

one, **G**

ber **F**

Num- **E**

E **F** **G**

two, **G** three, four, five,

ber **F** ber ber ber

num- **E** num- num- num- num-

Oh, **C′** Oh, **C′**

my! **C** my! **C**

C **C**

Music by You

42   MARIN, John. Circus Elephants 19″h x 24¾″w. The Alfred Steiglitz
Collection and Robert A. Waller Fund. THE ART INSTITUTE OF
CHICAGO.

I put my arms up high,
I put my arms down low,
I reach them to the sky,
then let them fall be - low.

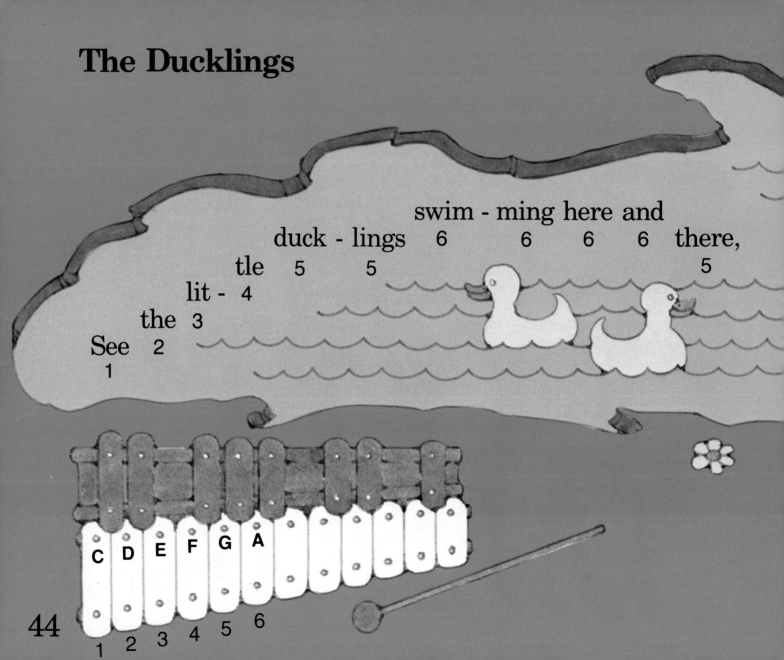

Heads are in the
4   4   4   4   wa - ter,
            3   3   Tails are in the
              2   2   2   2   air.
                     1

Congo Lullaby

Dance!

The Angel Band

D E G   G   D E G   G   D E G   B B   B A

There was one, there were two, there were three lit - tle an - gels,
There were four, there were five, there were six lit - tle an - gels,
There were seven, there were eight, there were nine lit - tle an - gels,

Ten lit - tle an - gels in that band.

49

REPETITION: Pitch Patterns

Make Up Silly Questions

QUESTION-AND-ANSWER PHRASES

Bell Talk

What If?

Great Big Bear

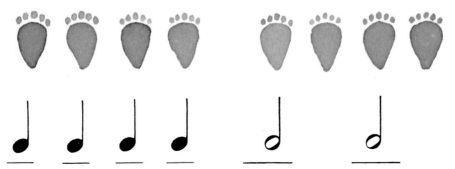

The Bus

The people on the bus go up and down

The wheels on the bus go round and round

SINGING ABOUT TRAVEL: Rhythm and Pitch

The peo-ple on the bus go up and down,

D' B G

up and down, up and down. The peo-ple on the bus go

up and down all through the town.

D' B G

55

Black and Gold

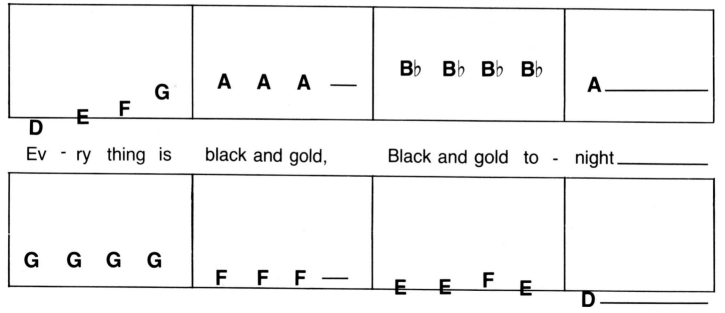

D E F G	A A A —	B♭ B♭ B♭ B♭	A_____
Ev - ry thing is	black and gold,	Black and gold to - night_____	

G G G G	F F F —	E E F E	D_____
Yel - low pump - kins,	yel - low moon,	yel - low can - dle - light._____	

Grandma Moses: OVER THE RIVER TO GRANDMA'S HOUSE ON
THANKSGIVING DAY. Copyright © 1979 Grandma Moses
Properties, Inc.

Candles of Hanukah

Burn, lit - tle can - dles, burn, burn, burn. Ha - nu - kah is here.

Burn, lit - tle can - dles, burn, burn, burn. Burn so bright and clear.

58

I Saw Three Ships

<pre>
      1   2   3   4
I saw three ships come sail - ing in,

          5   5   5   5
On Christ - mas Day, on Christ - mas Day.

      1   2   3   4
I saw three ships come sail - ing in,

          5   5   5   1
On Christ - mas Day in the morn - ing.
</pre>

59

Star Wishes

Star, oh, star
So brightly shining
Give my wish to me—
As we hang our wishing cards—
On the wishing tree.

Ta - na - ba - ta   ma - tsu - ri - no   na - tsu - no - yo - ru

Tan —   za - ku   So —   e - te   i - wa - i - ma   sho.

America

AUTHORS

Mary Val Marsh has been a member of the Music Education faculty of San Diego State University and is well known as a workshop clinician. She has had extensive experience teaching and supervising classroom music at every level from kindergarten through graduate school and is the author of *Choruses and Carols, Here a Song, There a Song,* and *Explore and Discover Music.*

Carroll A. Rinehart, Coordinator of Elementary Music, Tucson, Arizona, has served as a consultant and workshop clinician on the Manhattanville Music Curriculum Project. He is the author of four choral collections.

Edith J. Savage, Professor of Music, San Diego State University, has taught and supervised classroom teachers of music at every level from kindergarten through graduate school. She is the co-author of *Teaching Children to Sing,* and co-author of *First Experience in Music,* a college text for elementary teachers.

CONSULTANTS

William Brohn, consultant in rock and popular music, is a conductor, performer, and arranger in New York City.

Venoris Cates, consultant in Afro-American music, is a music supervisor in the Chicago Public Schools and has had long experience teaching music in elementary schools.

Wayne Johnson, musicology consultant, is Chairman of the Department of Music, Georgetown College, Georgetown, Ky.

Walter E. Purdy, consultant in music education, is Coordinator of Music Education, University of Houston.

John Rouillard, consultant in American Indian music, is a member of a Sioux tribe. He is in charge of the program of Indian studies, San Diego State University.

Jose Villarino, consultant in Mexican-American music, is an Assistant Professor of Mexican-American studies, San Diego State University.

David L. Wilmot, general consultant on the Teacher's Annotated Edition, is a Professor of Music Education, University of Florida at Gainesville.

Acknowledgments   continued from page ii

General Music Co., Inc. for "The Little White Duck" by Bernard Zaritsky and Walt Barrows. Copyright © General Music Publishing Co., Inc.

Ginn and Company for "The Bus" from *Singing on Our Way* of OUR SINGING WORLD series, © Copyright, 1959, 1957, 1949, by Ginn and Company. (Xerox Corporation). Used with permission.

Harcourt Brace Jovanovich, Inc. for "By'm Bye." From THE AMERICAN SONGBAG by Carl Sandburg, copyright 1927, by Harcourt Brace Jovanovich, Inc.; renewed, 1955, by Carl Sandburg. Reprinted and recorded by permission of the publishers.

Onga Ku No Toma Suzuki, for "Hoshimatsuri" (*Star Wishes*), music by Yutaka Suzuki, words by Tadamasa Yamamoto. Copyright by ONGAKU NO TOMO SHA CORP., Tokyo and reprinted by their permission.

G. Schirmer, Inc. for "The Angel Band" from 36 SOUTH CAROLINA SPIRITUALS by Carl Diton. Copyright 1930 by G. Schirmer, Inc. Used by permission.

Charles Scribner's Sons for "The Wolf." Reprinted with the permission of Charles Scribner's Sons from SONGS AND GAMES OF THE AMERICAS by Frank Henius. Copyright 1943 Charles Scribner's Sons.

Melvin Lee Steadman, Jr., for "Black and Gold" by Nancy Byrd Turner. Used by permission.

University Press of Virginia for "Down Came a Lady" from TRADITIONAL BALLADS OF VIRGINIA by Arthur Kyle Davis, Jr.

World Around Songs for "Ten Puppies" (Diez Perritos) from AMIGOS CANTANDO. Copyright © 1948, renewed 1976, Cooperative Recreation Service. By permission.

Instruments by The World of Peripole, Inc., Browns Mills, N.J. 08015.

Illustrated by Fred Harsh, Larry Mikec, Bill Morrison, Jan Pyk, Sally Springer, Lynn Titleman, Susan Vaeth, Justin Wager, Angela Adams, and Carol Gangemi
Photos by Ian Berry © 1970 Magnum Photos
Naurice Koonce, Norman Snyder, Clara Aich